FIGURES IN WOOD OF WEST AFRICA

STATUETTES EN BOIS
DE L'AFRIQUE OCCIDENTALE

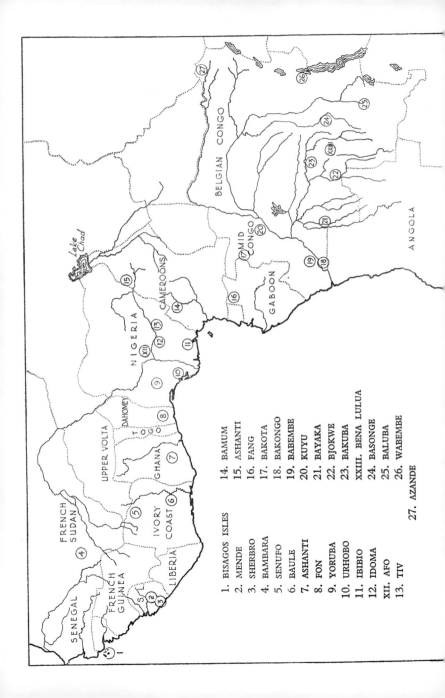

1. BISAGOS ISLES
2. MENDE
3. SHERBRO
4. BAMBARA
5. SENUFO
6. BAULE
7. ASHANTI
8. FON
9. YORUBA
10. URHOBO
11. IBIBIO
12. IDOMA
XII. AFO
13. TIV
14. BAMUM
15. ASHANTI
16. FANG
17. BAKOTA
18. BAKONGO
19. BABEMBE
20. KUYU
21. BAYAKA
22. BJOKWE
23. BAKUBA
XXIII. BENA LULUA
24. BASONGE
25. BALUBA
26. WABEMBE
27. AZANDE

FIGURES IN WOOD

OF WEST AFRICA

STATUETTES EN BOIS
DE L'AFRIQUE OCCIDENTALE

by

LEON UNDERWOOD

LONDON / **ALEC TIRANTI** / 1964

CONTENTS

First published 1947
Reprinted 1951, 1964

© ALEC TIRANTI LTD., 72 CHARLOTTE STREET, LONDON W.I.

MADE AND PRINTED IN THE UNITED KINGDOM

PREFACE

In writing of the art of West Africa, I have had prominently in mind the uncertainty about the meaning, in the twentieth century, of the term *primitive* applied to art. Our increased knowledge of the past has brought forth such a variety of elements in the make-up of 'primitive' that they exclude from its meaning any general association with crudeness. Elements like *naturalism*, as in prehistoric art, *schematism*, as in the art of the child and the bushman and *abstraction*, as in the art of the negro and others, require to be twisted into a single yarn of numerous strands from both past and present. The relationship of such varied elements in *primitive art* of the past has not been clarified by students of archæology and pre-history who, with scientific method, have discovered and preserved the earliest examples for us.

Only in the consciousness of the living artist may these separated elements be reunited. I, for instance, long interested in all forms of primitive art, see a connection between such various forms. They evolved in the changing habitat of the deity—the spiritual essence which prompts all artistic expression. The speculative opinions on the abstractions of West African art, expressed in these volumes, are based on this proposition. It may be very briefly stated as a transition in three degrees.

1

First, in the realistic primitive art of pre-historic times:

The deity, the force demanding artistic expression, resided in the object represented. The bison, for example, the subject of many cave drawings, was both worshipped and eaten.

Second, in the abstract primitive art of West Africa and elsewhere:

The invisible deity inhabiting a world of spirits, was *separate* from its artistic representation in the sensible world, yet associated with it.*

Third, the art of the present-day transition to a psychological degree of the Christian era:

The world of Spirits (in the second degree of transition) becomes depopulated and the deity resides in the individual conscience.

This hypothesis gives both the realism of palæolithic art and the abstraction or non-realism of West African art spiritual (religious) significance in different forms. In the representation of an unseen spirit in West Africa, a realistic likeness of its counterpart in the sensible world is not fitting; only sufficient resemblance is necessary to identify the one with the other. If this idea finds acceptance as a fair accounting for the abstract character of West African art, it is all that is required of it here. It may, however, be added that the appearance of naturalism in Greek art is to be regarded, not as a return to the first degree, but as a loss of abstraction in the second. The Greek's refinement of abstrac-

---

*Occasional ceremonial eating of the deity survives under totemism and, in symbolic form, in the Christian sacrament.

tion eventually defeated its own purpose, resulting in an expressionless naturalism. This was brought about by their awakening scientific knowledge and the increasing practice of mensuration, and was continued until expression was restored in Europe by the primitive reaction of the Romanesque and Byzantine styles.

ACKNOWLEDGMENTS

For permission to reproduce works and valuable assistance, acknowledgements and thanks are due to the Trustees of the British Museum, Horniman's Museum and The Royal Scottish Museum, and to Mr. R. P. Bedford, Mr. M. Cockin, Mr. W. B. Fagg, Mr. Rene d'Harnoncourt, Miss Gertrude Hermes, Mr. J. Keggie, Mr. W. O. Oldman, and Mr. B. Hughes-Stanton.

FIGURES IN WOOD
OF WEST AFRICA

The appeal of primitive art

THE art of West Africa has but recently freed itself from its protective chrysalis of ethnology in Europe, in which it lay secluded for so many years, and has made its appeal to the public on æsthetic grounds. Since its emergence from the museum glass case, in the last thirty years, the public has seen a good deal of it in art exhibitions and become aware of its influence upon European experimental art technique. Art tradition has in fact become for us more eclectic; to be drawn from wider sources in the past. The European's view of history is no longer what it was—confined to the narrow consideration of his own particular strain and descent, traced in the spoken and written word. He has now an added interest in the picture of his progenitors, outside the limited sphere of such evidence. Archæology and other sciences have helped to remove his bias of isolation. They may have widened his spiritual horizon but they have unsettled his spirit in doing so. They have shown him beneath the dust of the past other factors of more ultimate importance than the local struggles of despotic rulers which crowded his pages of history.*

* A few fragments of pre-historic sculpture were recovered from the debris smothering the hearths of pre-historic man: in 1909, at Willendorf, Austria, was found a small female figure (about 5 ins. high, in oolite limestone) of proportions considered grotesque and called 'steatopagus.' It was embedded 6 ft. from the surface in the loess of a railway cutting, near a charcoal hearth, and was considered to be of Aurignacian or Solutrian age—30,000 (?) years.

Dust has been wittily described as matter in the wrong place. Truant specks of significant ancient matter have been finding their way to the right place —in the service of man. How much of this reassortment of matter is due to the deliberate methods of science or to man's mere speculative belief is not being considered here; but where art has helped to model man in the past there can be little doubt that speculative belief has played a leading part. Unrecorded history, brought to light by science, shows a recurring pattern of man groping eternally amid the ashes on the hearth of his ancestors—in search of the Phœnix egg. Man's invention of the Phœnix myth itself, is evidence of his urge to search amid ancestral ashes. We may not question the importance of such restless activity in removing dust and debris from the art of remote antiquity. It can make only one point in the mystery of man's existence—his genius for observation in the pursuit of the sublime. Man in his passage from dust to dust periodically searched the ancestral piles for some lost grain to stimulate his new grasp at perfection. The artist of the West began to see the 'curios' of West Africa in a new light.

Past triumphs revealed by present difficulties.

During the last hundred years in Europe the technique of the visula arts has turned gradually from the classical precedent towards the primitive. In this turning away we are to note two impulses: first, in the break away from the old classical subject matter, a heightened naturalistic technique was attempted, on the lines of the new optical science, resulting in impressionism; second, when the possibilities of employing optical science in art were exhausted the artist became post-impressionist and turned his attention from science to the study of primitive art. His hunt for the Phœnix egg amid the ancestral ashes was renewed. The artist, as post-impressionist, studied the art of West Africa among that of other primitives. Impressionism had failed to occupy the place of discarded classical subject matter in art, with the new optical technique; but I have not space to elaborate this statement. We must regard impressionism and post-impressionism as impulses concerned with little more than technique— not as the theme of a fresh renaissance, but as the avoidance of old belief—as far as that was possible in the search for a new technique. Impressionism preserved the old classical standards of drawing, based upon an intellectual understanding of mensuration, but this too was banished under post-impressionism in its study of primitive art.* A yearning for subject matter, a regret at its absence, was clearly felt, but none could be found to embody its departed spirit.

Surrealism represents an attempt made to reinstate subject matter, in an emancipated form, by presenting the visual stuff that dreams are made of. It was presented with artificial juxtaposition, in imitation of that strange but logical confusion of the

* Abstraction in West African art and its distinction from the 'pure' abstraction in post-impressionism are discussed at more length in the volume on Masks.

subconscious mind, as expounded by analytical psychologists. But this ingenious simulation was too intellectual for picture making. The intellectual endowments of individuals in large communities are too unequal for a common appeal to be made via the intellect. Surrealism called for and largely produced a host of interpreters.

It has been necessary to state the foregoing very briefly to put us in touch with the significance of abstract form in West African art. For us as for the early impressionists African art may be seen intimately, in its primitive beauty and strength, through the spectacles of contemporary art. The outstanding distinction between the post-impressionist and the African, whose art he had begun to study, lay in the different position art occupied in their respective lives. Van Gogh and Gauguin, well aware of the wider appeal of the art of the primitive to his people, were unable to restore this appeal of art to the lives of their own people.

Realism and abstraction.

A simple and universal* faith finds expression in the carved figures of West Africa. The abstract treatment of form in African art is a survival of a more general prototype which, in Europe, lasted until early Greek art. It disappeared to reappear again in Romanesque and Byzantine art. In the Elgin marbles and African carvings in the British Museum may be seen two forms which sculpture has

* Universal within the confines of tribal culture and its influence.

given to diverging beliefs. Realism in Greek art reflects the intellectual development of the Greeks and its demand for more and more detailed comparison between sculptured form and natural form. The Greeks expressed the figure in its muscular complexities. They arrived at this by a reasoning observation of its surface subtleties, which anticipated the artist's study of anatomy. In early Greek art the head was expressive but in the later periods the body took precedence as the focal point of expression and the head became a placid mask. At this point late Greek and African art (considered as the prototype of early Greek) stand farthest apart. The African carver treats the form non-realistically and focuses expression in the head.* Logic and proportion have no part in his attainment of sculptural unity. The African carver derives all his forms from a close study of nature but he abstracts the forms of nature beyond an immediate or direct comparison with her models. His work possesses a unity of a different kind which I will call *pre-logical* for, unlike the Greek, it demands no confirmation by a logical comparison with nature's forms. Before leaving Greek sculpture it is as well to note that the most sculpturally eloquent of the Greek works are from the earlier periods when the sculptor was allowed more personal deviation from the measured ideal. In fact, the slavish perfection which was attained ultimately by mensuration in late examples took the life and expression from Greek art.

* Although the head is much enlarged as the focus of expression in African art, portraiture appears to have been introduced by foreign influence.

Abstraction of natural form, in some degree, may be considered as the *verb* of the sculptor's language. This variation from the natural form in the art of the past, either primitive or classical, Christian or pagan, is the something-in-common which links different examples, and makes more obvious differences superficial to them as works of art. The direct and pre-logical technique of the African carver, dealing in abstract form with the subject matter of common belief, gave it an appeal to the hearts of the many as well as the heads of the few. Lost as mere 'fetish figures' in a more material world, African work depended for its rediscovery as works of art upon a bridging of the gap between European and African ideas, involving a less stigmatic interpretation of the word *primitive*.

By looking at it along with the art of Greece, and through the contemporary looking-glass which has already become primitive-tinted, we may see what to expect from the art of West Africa.

African art and religion.

In the volume on *The Masks of West Africa* I have said that the carved representations of nothing but a colony of spirits have come to be regarded, by our less credulous selves, as works of art. A lucidity suffuses works done under the persuasion of a belief. It is something which is added to the spiritual meaning of the belief, and survives it in works which afterwards rank as world masterpieces. The significance they acquired as religious expression becomes transmuted into significance as works of art, long after the dogma and doctrine of their originating belief have passed into oblivion. Regarded in this way, as the documents of the essence of a forgotten belief,* works of art leave their natal environment of particular dogma and doctrine behind.

As this principle of contiguity seems unquestionable in art of no matter what origin, it may not be out of place to give a couple of quotations typical of conflicting views about the value of belief in connection with primitive art. The first is by Professor Olbrechts, Curator of the Ethnographical Museum of Ghent, who writes:

' A great deal of æsthetic satisfaction can be got from the mere contemplation of primitive works of art, without regard to their origin or social function.' He adds to this: 'Our æsthetic joy may be greatly increased by the study of the life and customs that gave these works their existence.'

But woe to those who in sympathy should turn for further enlightenment on the life and customs to Frazer's *Golden Bough*, on which he spent so many years of his life collecting, sifting and arranging primitive customs and beliefs. In his preface to *Aftermath*, supplement to *The Golden Bough*, he says:

'I was beguiled, as by some subtle enchanter, into inditing what I cannot but regard as a dark, a tragic chronicle of human error and folly, fruitless endeavour, wasted time and blighted hopes.' He concludes: '. . . at the best the chronicle may serve as a warning, as a sort of Ariadne's thread, to help the forlorn wayfarer to shun some of the snares and

* Forgotten for Europeans; perhaps, unrealisable. Rattray says some Ashanti words have meanings which are untranslatable

Rattray—*Ashanti*.

pitfalls into which his fellows have fallen before him in the labyrinth of life.'

Yet, in the presence of the very real æsthetic pleasure we receive from West African art, we cannot abandon Professor Olbrecht's hope, for Frazer's despair. We have to decide that even if the beliefs and customs of primitive man be found wrong, his faith in himself expressed in his art is right, no matter how inadequately this faith may be expressed in his customs and beliefs. The æsthetic pleasure his art gives must remain a mystery between ourselves and art, and not confused with the conditions of its background. For only if these two remain distinct (the constancy of art and the changeableness of life) have we any prospect of reconciling the opposed views (hope and despair) on the value of art of the past.

Religious and pure abstraction

These works retain their æsthetic significance even though the customs and beliefs are dead which gave rise to the works. So dogma and doctrine, of whatever kind, seem unimportant so long as belief is present. An abstract belief without dogma and doctrine was not possible for African man nor, if it had been, would it have given his art both individual expression and a common appeal and bound his people together in tribal life. Individual expression and common appeal are the attributes of any great and enduring art. Notwithstanding its gloomy imperfections of custom and belief, African society was a fellowship founded near to the earth. Speaking of sacred groves, Frazer says:

'All this, the grove, the tree and the stone represent the EARTH, the sacred mother of all things.'

In the Shongo cult of the Yorubas, at one time a tribe of the most extensive influence in Nigeria, the motif most frequently addressed by the carver to the spirits controlling fertility is Mother and Child—MOTHER EARTH feeding mankind. Every tribal African identifies himself with mankind, the animals and even trees, as children of the earth. It is not difficult to accept the value of belief to the tribal African, for it is impossible to conceive what he would have done about life without it even had he known his dogma and doctrine were shortly to be discredited. The carver contributed vital expression to this belief. In a language of common currency he created an imagery representing the spirits controlling fertility, a first principle in the well-being of himself, his family and tribe.

In the case of the Christian, his faith is itself an abstract, withdrawing control from the spirits of primitive faith, and placing it largely in the believer's conscience. It calls for a representation by art of the ideal type of human, to house the abstract ideal *conscience*. Its Madonnas are representations of ideal woman, not spirits. Religion and art for the primitive are parts of life not to be considered separately. The business of art for him is to represent or mirror with common appeal the unseen world of spirits in their separate characters and identities controlling man's well-being in the fertility of the earth. Woman representing Mother Earth is portrayed with the humility of the *vulgar* type, not the ideal.*

* See plate 16.

In such a setting, abstract art like pure 'music' of the West could have no existence as a creative product separate from the common touch and appeal. The Western idea of 'pure' abstraction in the visual arts arises from the intellectual promotion of the spirits controlling Africa, to atoms and electrons going about their legitimate impersonal business, in control of an impersonal universe.

Logically enough, a tribal African does not offend his conscience in transgressing his belief, but the spirits of the unseen world, whose offence if unchecked would provoke them to take revenge upon him, his family or whole tribe. The external world has been denuded of spirits by Western man who has included all their spiritual values in his conscience. Their common appeal has been lost in the vagueness of their abstract identities in conscience. The leprechauns may still visit the Irish but they are no longer sufficiently feared and respected to be honoured with creative expression. It seems clear that faith must be held with an esteem as moving as love and fear for it to produce a religious art in which the creative energy, controlled by emotional gears, has a common appeal—no matter what direction it is given by thought.

Antiquity, climate, materials, tradition.

The question of the age of works is a difficult one in the general obscurity of the 'dark continent.' Roger Bacon said that there is only one darkness and that is ignorance. In a territory which is without written records and in which mention of a military defeat was forbidden on pain of death, no chronological order may be given to works of art. African art therefore has to be seen in the same way as prehistoric; without centuries and decades, in terms of evolution.*

The vast area of the scene, profuse in animal life and vegetation is inhabited by man at an advanced stage of primitive development. Friendly climate and fertility of the soil have a restraining influence upon the development of the inhabitants. Agriculture made an advance but domestication of cattle was prevented by the tse-tse fly. On the tribal scale there have been innumerable stirrings and fermentations, liberating and suppressing in turn various internal influences. Africa absorbed all external influences without losing much to any of them, before the penetration by Western science and industrialism. A degree of immunity to malaria was acquired by the inhabitants, greatly assisting their defence against foreign invaders. The archæologist finds surprises which suggest intrusions and foreign influences that have vanished beyond other trace.†

The humidity of the climate is corrosive to all materials, and the white ant is a rapid destroyer of wood. It is unfortunate that wood should be the staple material of the carver and the diet of the white ant in a country which has no readily work-

* The attempt made by a Parisian dealer, to date works in terms of centuries, must be regarded as purely fanciful where it is not established upon European influence.

† The bronze heads of Ife; steatite figures of Essie and terracottas of Jemme, to mention Nigeria alone.

able stone. But this fact may have helped in preserving the art of ancestor worshippers from the static style of stone. The perishable condition of wood, allowing no work to become a fixed example for over-long, assisted the dynamic variety of style so characteristic of West African art. But it is questionable if tribal life in small units would have submitted to a static tradition, even had it suited the temperament of the African. A plentiful supply of durable stone would nevertheless have had some influence in binding a style which we find so free. For had, let us say, the porphyry sculptures of Egypt crumbled away every few years under the attentions of climate and white ant, no gigantic pharaohs would have stood in the deserts, prohibiting for dynasties any but the most superficial variations in Egypt's great and revered ancestral style. The extraordinary versatility of African carvings, though in the greater part due to the character of the race, must have found some support in the corruptibility of the limited materials.

African abstraction of form.

I can find no better term for the abstraction in negro sculpture than 'pre-logical' form. Whatever the term employed it must also be valid for that abstraction found in its incipient form in children's drawings. The adult negro preserves the child's initial impulse for self expression. Children's drawings have a disarming simplicity like the humanity of negro work. They share a freedom from self-consciousness, though neither child nor negro thinks the sensible world surrounding him looks like his representations. *Except ye become as little children* —without innocence, the unquestioning simplicity of a child, undue regard will be paid to those non-essentials that frustrate the expression of faith. Roger Fry says in his *Art of the Bushmen**:

'The primitive drawing of our race is singularly like that of children. Its most striking peculiarity is the extent to which it is dominated by concepts of the language. In a child's drawing we find a number of forms which have scarcely any reference to actual appearances, but which directly symbolise the most significant concepts of the thing represented. For a child a man is the sum concept of the head (which in turn consists of eyes, nose and mouth), of his arms, his hands (five fingers), his legs and his feet. Torso is not a concept which interests him, and it is, therefore, usually reduced to a single line which seems to link the concept-symbol head with those of legs. The child does, of course, know that the figure thus drawn is not like man, but it is a kind of hieroglyphic script for man, and satisfies his desire for expression.'

We must acknowledge Fry's shrewd observations on the similarity between the drawings of the child and the bushman. The bushman and the child draw in a style known as schematism. This may be explained, as Fry suggests, as a sort of abbreviated naturalism or shorthand statement—'hieroglyphic script.' It must not be confused with the negro abstraction which I have called pre-logical form, The negro's treatment of the torso is as direct as the child's drawing of the head (eyes, nose and mouth) but it is not so simple and crude. He is interested in

* *The Art of the Bushmen—Vision and Design*, by Roger Fry. An article reprinted from the BURLINGTON MAGAZINE, 1910.

those features of the *torso* giving expression to his belief: the navel—the cord of life; the mother's out-thrusting breasts—sustainers of infant life; the pubis —the portal of life and, the cicatrices and tribal markings on the body—his passport to join the spirits of his tribal companions in the life after death. With these features duly emphasised by enlargement and simplification he seeks to give the torso the divine aspect of the threshold of the super-natural world. The plain surfaces of the torso and the limbs have no meaning for him, with their subtle surface undulations. His only use of these parts is to reduce them to assist in the expression of the capital features, bringing them into a new unity as a representation of a spirit, in which he sees the supernatural world reflected in the sensible.

A child knows nothing of the features of the torso. He draws the sense organs of the head because for him they represent the mysterious sensible world he is entering gradually with the aid of adults. The child would not mistake the face of another for his mother's. He is aware of the subtler features of the head but they have as yet no meaning for him. The European child soon acquires a conscience to deal with the spirits inhabiting the negro's world of belief. In his interest in fairy tales and in his private moments with his young companions he shows the old inherited disposition to people the sensible world about him with spirits. Neither child nor negro carver is intellectually interested in form, otherwise they could not use it so freely nor would they care so little for the fate of their finished work. The child discards and destroys his work, and the primitive that of his defeated enemies—no matter what æsthetic merit it possesses. Yet the negro's carving could not surpass the child's drawing in completeness or finality, as it does, if he had not *some* interest in form. The nature of his intimacy with form is perhaps best described by an analogy. To him, form is a token of indirect value—much in the same way as we consider the formula in making out bank cheques; extremely important in every detail but of no value unless there is credit to meet the draft. No one, outside a school of accountancy, makes out and receives bank cheques for the sake of their appearance. Bank cheques become our *fetish*—as carving, for the negro—but never our idol. Negro art is a creative representation like the drawing of the child which has for a time the power to stimulate his grasp at something unseen by an abstraction of something seen.

When form is employed in the indirect manner of the child, the negro carver and our bankers, all its values are pressed into the service of expression. No self-conscious technique is permitted to divert the urgency of expression. The grammarians of form (to paraphrase a term from the study of languages*) come later to make it a self-conscious technique with hair-splitting shades of meaning. This happens when the fire of the first purpose is down to embers.

* *Philology*—the study of languages in connection with the whole moral and intellectual action of the peoples using them; but the most common meaning now is science of language; linguistic science; often expressed by the comparative title of *comparative philology* (Concise English Dictionary). The intellectual study of form becomes as detached from the urgency of its original use in art as it does in languages.

18

The African school.

The art schools of West Africa were its secret societies. Captain F. W. Butt-Thompson says of them in his *West African Secret Societies:*

'They were instituted to enforce and maintain tribal traditions, customs and beliefs that were in danger of changing or becoming obsolete. The organisers were champions of the old against the new, as some of their descendants still are. They were restrictors of mental advance and punishers of the heretic and the unorthodox. They were clever enough to know that prohibition alone was not sufficient foundation for any society desiring longevity, and, therefore, made their societies the repositories of folk-lore, myths and histroy and the conceptions of art and culture and learning and wisdom the tribe possessed. Moreover, they became the teachers of these things. The only teachers.'

Primitive institutions such as these first conserved the arts and developed them by organising their common appeal. Art flourished under them as long as their powers of conservatism expanded, but when their expansion ceased and conservatism became absolute and static, art declined. The axiom of their wisdom was to interpret and impersonate the spirits of the unseen world in a form of belief which survived long in the isolation of Africa. Art expressed their religious emotions in organised and restrained form.

Early European adventurers who went to West Africa found art in full flower of expression, which they did not understand. They and the early missionaries saw nothing of value in pagan ways and beliefs comparable to Christianity and much was destroyed in the zeal of punishment and conversion. No constructive comment may be made upon that. What was preserved for curiosity or scientific interest had long to wait in Europe—for a more eclectic meaning in tradition—before it was to receive any recognised spiritual significance there. Europe's economic penetration of Africa short-circuited any further evolution. Who can say if the West Africa of the future—its people equipped with a European conscience, in place of a host of spirit mentors—will find a new form of artistic expression?

The carver's knowledge of form was confined to its volume and surface. He knew how to make his material* express the emotions of his simple belief. We do not find him attempting in his figures the exploration of space by an arrangement of his forms on a spiral axis; the spines of his figures are never represented in rotation, giving all views (front, side and back) a variety of outline.† He seldom turns the head upon the neck. His carvings present but two views in contour, front and side. Curiously, and perhaps significantly, the child, in carvings of *Mother and Child*, is an exception. In works from both Yorubaland and the Belgian Congo, the child is represented in a freer attitude in contrast to the

* Most of their work was in wood, the subject of this volume, but they had the same sympathy for all materials in which they worked.

† Some notable exceptions to this observation are the stone figures (steatite 'nomalies' and rice gods) of Sierra Leone. They are of ancient origin and probably of foreign influence. Other exceptions such as the Portuguese riflemen and archebusiers in bronze from Benin, are also accepted as in an introduced style.

straight uprightness of its mother. Generally speaking, the rigidity of posture in African carvings leaves all suggestions of movement to the subtle variation of forms and surfaces.

The cosmogony of primitive Africa does not extend to the free spaces beyond its tropical forests and above its moody blue and leaden sky, which is regarded as a solid plane—a ceiling. Africa, in its art, reflected the limited boundaries of its sensible world; back, front and sides of figures—the four winds; the feet and head—earth and sky. The unseen places in which the African's spirit may have roamed did not call upon his imagination to explore them in sculptural form.

SHORT BIBLIOGRAPHY.

ART, ILLUSTRATED.

Kjersmeir, Carl, *Centres de Style de la Sculpture Africaine.* Paris, 1945.

Sweeney, J. J., *African Negro Art.* N.Y., 1935.

Maes, J. et Lavachery, H., *Art Nègre.* Brussels, 1930.

Herskovito, Melville J., *The Background of African Art.* Denver, U.S.A.

Guillaume, Paul and Munro, Thomas, *Negro Sculpture.* 1926.

Portier and Poncetton, *Les Arts Sauvages Afrique.*

Einstein, *La Sculpture Africaine.* Paris, 1920.

Olbrechts: Foreword, Primitive Art Exhibition, Berkeley Gallery, June, 1947.

Underwood, Leon, *Masks of West Africa.* 1947.

ETHNOLOGICAL.

Dennett, R. E., *Nigerian Studies. At the Back of the Black Man's Mind.*

Rattray, Ashanti, *Religion and Art of the Ashanti.*

Fraser, J. G., *The Golden Bough.*

Monod, Th., *Au bord de l'Ocean Ténébreux; Atlantic et Afrique.* I.F.A.N.

Spearing: *The Childhood of Art.*

Burton, R. F.: *Notes on Certain Matters Connected with the Dahoman.* MEMOIRS—ANTHROPOLOGICAL SOCIETY, Vol. 1, No. 10. 1863.

BULLETINS OF L'INSTITUT FRANÇAIS D'AFRIQUE NOIR. *Notes Africaines.* Dakar.

GENERAL.

Kingsley, Mary, *West African Studies, travels in West Africa.* 1897.

Clarke, J. D., *Omu: An Educational Experiment.*

Gorer, G., *Africa Dances.* London.

Frobenius, L., *Africa Genesis.* (Translations of Folk Lore).

Gorvie, Max, *Old and New in Sierra Leone.*

D'Albeca, A. L., *La France au Dahomey.*

Fry, Roger, *Vision and Design.*

PREFACE

En traitant de l'Art de l'Afrique Occidentale, j'ai eu particulièrement présent à l'esprit le vague qui, au XXeme siècle, s'attache au sens du terme *primitif*, appliqué à l'art. Notre connaissance accrue du passé a fait éclore une telle variété d'éléments dans la conception du mot *primitif* qu'ils excluent de son sens toute association avec la grossièreté. Des éléments, comme le *naturalisme* dans l'art préhistorique, le *schématisme* dans l'art chez l'enfant et l'homme des forêts, et *l'abstraction*, par exemple dans l'art nègre et d'autres encore, demandent à être tissés tels les fils d'une même toile, comprenant à la fois le passé et le présent. Les rapports entre des éléments si variés dans l'art primitif ancien n'ont pas été éclaircis par les étudiants de l'archéologie et de la préhistoire qui, à l'aide de la méthode scientifique, en ont découvert et conservi pour nous les tout premiers exemples.

C'est seulement dans la conscience de l'artiste vivant que ces éléments séparés peuvent être réunis. Pour moi, par exemple, qui m'intéresse depuis longtemps à toutes les formes de l'art primitif, il existe un rapport entre des formes si variées. Elles ont évolué suivant les modifications de l'habitat de la divinité: essence spirituelle qui inspire toute expression artistique. Les spéculations sur les abstractions de l'Art de l'Afrique Occidentale, exprimées dans ces pages, sont basées sur cette proposition: très brièvement, on peut la considerer comme une transition opérée en trois stages.

Premièrement, l'art primitif réaliste des temps préhistoriques. La divinité qui exigeait une expression artistique, résidait dans l'objet représenté. Par exemple, le bison, sujet de nombreux dessins de grotte, était à la fois adoré et mangé.

Deuxièment, l'art primitif abstrait de l'Afrique Occidentale et d'ailleurs. La divinité invisible qui habite le monde des esprits était distincte de la représentation artistique du monde sensible et cependant lui était associée.*

---

* La manducation solennelle et occasionnelle de la divinité survit dans le totémisme et, sous une forme symbolique, dans le sacrement chrétien.

Troisèment, l'art contemporain qui, psychologiquement parlant, est en transition avec l'ère chrétienne. Le monde des esprits (celui du deuxième degré de transition) se dépeuple et la divinité réside dans la conscience individuelle. Cette hypothèse revêt à la fois le réalisme de l'art paléolithique et l'abstraction ou l'absence de réalisme dans l'Art de l'Afrique Occidentale d'un sens spirituel, c'est-à-dire religieux qui prend différentes formes.

Pour représenter un esprit invisible de l'Afrique Occidentale une ressemblance réaliste de sa contre-partie dans le monde sensible ne convient pas; seulement une ressemblance suffisante est nécessaire à les identifier. Si on trouve que cette idée fournisse une explication acceptable du caractère abstrait de l'Art de l'Afrique Occidentale, c'est tout ce qui est requis ici.

Il est cependant possible d'ajouter que l'aspect naturaliste de l'art grec doit être regardé non comme un retour du premier stage, mais comme une diminution de l'abstraction du second. Le raffinement de l'abstraction chez les Grecs déjoua son dessein et eut pour résultat le naturalisme dénué de toute expression. Celui-ci fut amené par l'éveil de leurs connaissances scientifiques et la pratique croissante de la mensuration, et se poursuivit jusqu'à ce que l'expression retrouvât sa place en Europe dans la réaction primitive des styles Roman et Byzantin.

L'attrait de l'art primitif.

L'ART de l'Afrique Occidentale ne s'est libéré que récemment en Europe de la chrysalide protectrice de l'ethnologie dans laquelle il reposait depuis tant d'années, et a exercé un attrait sur le public pour des raisons esthétiques. Depuis son émergence de la vitrine de musée pendant les trente dernières années, de nombreuses expositions en furent faites, et le public s'est rendu compte de l'influence que cet art exerce sur l'art technique et expérimental européen. La tradition artistique est en fait devenue plus éclectique, et a été tirée d'un passé aux sources plus larges. L'Européen considère maintenant l'histoire sous un autre jour. Il ne la confine plus a l'étude étroite de sa propre descendance et des traits qui lui sont particuliers, étude basée sur le langage parlé et écrit; mais son intérêt s'accroît maintenant de la connaissance de l'image de ses ancêtres, hors de la sphère limitée de cette évidence. L'archéologie et les autres sciences ont contribué à lui ôter tout sens d'isolement. Mais tout en élargissant son horizon spirituel elles ont jeté le trouble dans son esprit. Sous la poussière du passé elles lui ont révélé d'autres facteurs d'une importance ultime plus grande que les luttes régionales entre des chefs despotiques qui remplissent les pages de son histoire.* On a défini avec esprit que la poussière était de la matière au mauvais endroit. Les petits grains vagabonds, molécules de poussière ancienne chargées de sens, ont trouvés leur propre endroit enfin—au service de l'homme. Dans ce réajustement de la matière, quelle part revient aux méthodes délibérées de la science ou à la simple croyance spéculative de l'homme, il n'entre pas dans notre sujet de le dire, mais là où l'art a contribué à façonner l'homme dans le passé on ne peut mettre en doute que la croyance spéculative ait joué une part importante. Des vestiges de l'histoire, mis à jour par la science, révèlent un certain schéma récurrent qui montre l'homme, tâtonnant éternellement parmi les cendres du foyer de ses ancêtres— à la recherche de l'œuf du Phœnix. L'invention même du mythe du Phœnix est l'évidence du désir puissant de l'homme à fouiller dans les cendres ancestrales. Nous n'avons pas le droit de mettre en question l'importance de cette activité incessante, livrée à enlever la poussière qui recouvre les ruines de l'art des époques les plus reculées. Cette activité révèle seulement une chose dans le mystère de l'existence de

* Des fragments de sculpture préhistorique ont été découverts sous les débris qui couvraient les foyers de l'homme préhistorique: en 1909, à Willendorf en Autriche, on trouva une petite statue de femme (d'environ cinq pouces de haut, en calcaire oolithique) de proportions considérées comme grotesques, et appelée *steatopage*. Elle était enfouie à six pieds de profondeur, dans le remblai d'une voie ferrée, près d'un foyer de charbon de bois. On pense qu'elle remontait à l'âge d'Aurignac ou de Solutre (30,000 ans avant J. C. ?).

l'homme: son génie d'observation dans la poursuite du sublime. L'homme qui est poussière et retourne à la poussière a remué périodiquement les amoncellements de l'antiquité pour y trouver quelque grain de poussière égarée qui puisse le pousser à s'emparer d'une perfection nouvelle. L'artiste de l'occident commence à considérer sous un nouveau jour *les objets d'art bizarres* de l'Afrique Occidentale.

Les triomphes du passé sont révélés par les difficultés présentes.

Pendant les cent dernières années en Europe, la technique des arts visuels s'est orientée graduellement du précédent de l'époque classique à celui de l'époque primitive. Dans cette nouvelle orientation il faut noter deux impulsions. Premièrement, la rupture d'avec le sujet classique ancien fut suivie d'un effort vers une technique naturaliste perfectionnée, suivant la voie de la nouvelle science optique: le résultat en fut l'impressionnisme. Secondement, lorsque l'artiste eut épuisé tous les usages possibles de l'optique, il devint postimpressionniste et tourna alors son attention vers l'étude de l'art primitif. Sa recherche assidue de l'œuf du Phœnix au milieu des cendres millénaires fut renouvellée. L'artiste postimpressionniste étudia l'art de l'Afrique Occidentale entre autres arts primitifs. Dans le domaine de l'art, l'impressionnisme, aidé de la méthode de la science optique, avait échoué à prendre la place du sujet classique alors écarté, mais je n'ai pas la place ici d'élaborer cette déclaration. Nous devons regarder l'impressionnisme et le postimpressionnisme comme des mouvements touchant les chose guère plus profondes que la technique—et non comme le thème d'une innovation mais plutôt comme un désir de fuir une croyance ancienne dans la recherche d'une nouvelle technique. L'impressionnisme conserva les règles classiques de dessin, fondées sur une compréhension de la mensuration, mais celles-ci furent rejetées par le postimpressionnisme après l'étude que fit ce mouvement de primitif.* Les adeptes de ce mouvement éprouvaient le désir

* Voir le volume sur les *Masques* pour un essai plus complet sur l'abstraction dans l'art de l'Afrique occidentale, et sa différence de l'abstraction *pure* du post-impressionisme.

d'un sujet et en regrettaient l'absence, mais n'en purent trouver qui remplaçât l'inspiration envolée.

Le surréalisme représente un effort vers la restauration d'un sujet, sous une forme émancipée, par la présentation visuelle de ce dont sont faits les rêves. Cette présentation était opérée par une juxtaposition artificielle qui imitait la confusion étrange mais logique du subconscient telle qu'elle est exposée par les psychanalystes. Mais ce déguisement ingénieux etait trop intellectuel pour produire des tableaux. Les dons intellectuels des individus des groupes importants de la société sont trop inégaux pour qu'on puisse faire appel au groupe par l'intermédiaire de l'intelligence. Le surréalisme nécessitait et suscita surtout des légions d'interprètes.

Ce préambule était nécessaire pour nous faire sentir la signification de la forme abstraite de l'art de l'Afrique Occidentale. Pour nous comme pour les tout premiers impressionnistes l'art africain peut être vu intimement dans sa beauté et sa puissance primitives, dans le miroir de l'art contemporain. La distinction majeure entre le post-impressionniste et l'africain (dont celui-là avait commencé à étudier l'art) réside dans la position différente que l'art occupait dans leurs vies respectives. Van Gogh et Paul Ganguin, conscients de l'attrait plus général de l'art primitif pour son peuple ne purent pas élargir cet attrait de l'art dans la vie de leurs propres compatriotes.

Réalisme et abstraction.

C'est une foi simple et universelle* qui trouve son expression dans les statues sculptées de l'Afrique Occidentale. Le traitement abstrait d'une forme chez l'africain est une survivance d'un prototype plus général qui, en Europe, dura jusqu'à l'art primitif grec. Il disparut pour reparaître à nouveau dans l'art Roman et l'art Byzantin. Sur les marbres d'Elgin et sur les sculptures africaines du British Museum on peut voir deux formes données par la sculpture à deux croyances divergentes.

* Universel a l'intérieur de la zone de culture de la tribe et de son influence.

Le réalisme de l'art grec reflète le développement intellectuel des Grecs qui exigeait une comparaison de plus en plus détaillée entre la forme sculptée et la forme naturelle. Les Grecs exprimaient les complexités musculaires du corps humain; ils y atteignirent par l'observation raisonnée des toutes les subtilités extérieures de forme qui anticipaient l'étude de l'anatomie par l'artiste. Dans l'art primitif grec la tête était expressive, mais plus tard le corps prit précédence et devint le point central d'expression alors que la tête devenait un masque placide. C'est à ce point-là que l'art grec avancé et l'art africain (considéré comme le prototype de l'art primitif grec) sont le plus éloignés l'un de l'autre. Le sculpteur africain traite la forme d'une manière non réaliste et centralise l'expression sur la tête.* La logique et les proportions n'ont aucune part dans sa réalisation de l'unité sculpturelle. Le sculpteur africain tire toutes ses formes d'une étude approfondie de la nature, mais il en tire une abstraction qui dépasse toute comparaison immédiate ou directe avec les modèles de la nature. Son œuvre possède une unité d'une espèce différente que j'appelerai *pre-logique* car, contrairement à l'œuvre grecque elle n'exige aucune confirmation apportée par la comparaison logique avec les formes naturelles. Avant de quitter la sculpture grecque, il est bon de faire remarquer que les plus éloquentes œuvres de sculpture grecque sont celles des époques primitives, époques où l'on permettait à chaque artiste individuellement de dévier davantage de l'idéal établi. En fait, la perfection servile atteinte en dernier lieu grâce à la mensuration dans les derniers exemples de sculpture de l'art grec, lui enleva toute vie et toute expression.

Ce procédé d'abstraction opéré sur une forme naturelle peut en quelque sorte être considéré comme le *verbe* du langage du sculpteur. Cette variation de la forme naturelle dans l'art du passé, qu'il soit primitif ou classique, chrétien ou païen, est le facteur commun qui lie entre eux des exemples différents et rend superficielles des différences plus évidentes entre ces œuvres, en tant qu'œuvres d'art. La technique

* La tête des statues étant de proportions exagérées, en tant que centre d'expression dans l'art africain, le portrait semble avoir été introduit par une influence étrangère.

directe et prélogique du sculpteur africain qui s'occupait sous une forme abstraite du sujet de croyance commun à tous, lui attirait tous les cœurs aussi bien que les têtes de quelques uns. Egarées et traitées de simples fétiches dans un monde plus matérialiste, les œuvres africaines dépendaient, pour être reconnues comme œuvres d'art, d'un trait d'union entre les concepts européens et africains impliquant une interprétation moins stigmatisante du mot *primitif*. En étudiant cette œuvre parallèlement à l'art de la Grèce, et à travers le miroir contemporain qui s'est déjà ombré d'art primitif, on peut deviner ce qu'est l'art de l'Afrique Occidentale.

L'art et la religion africain.

Dans le volume sur les masques de l'Afrique Occidentale, j'ai dit que les représentations sculptées d'une colonie d'esprits sont maintenant considérées par nos âmes moins crédules comme des œuvres d'art. Une certaine lucidité baigne les œuvres inspirées par la foi. C'est quelque chose qui s'ajoute à la signification spirituelle de la croyance et qui survit dans des œuvres qui après, occupent leur rang parmi les chefs-d'œuvres du monde. Le sens qu'elles acquièrent en tant que symboles d'une foi religieuse, se transmue en sens artistique, longtemps après que sont oubliés le dogme et la doctrine qui leur ont donné naissance. Vues sous cet angle-là, comme des documents de l'essence d'une croyance oubliée* les œuvres d'art laissent loin derrière elles leur milieu originel, leur dogme et leur doctrine particuliers. Comme le principe de contiguïté semble indiscutable dans tout art—quelle que soit son origine —il n'est peut-être pas déplacé de faire deux citations typiques d'opinions contradictoires sur la valeur de la croyance par rapport à l'art primitif.

La première est du professeur Olbrechts, conservateur du Musée Ethnographique de Gand, qui écrit: 'on peut tirer beaucoup de plaisir esthétique à la simple contemplation d'œuvres d'art primitif, sans tenir compte de leur origine ou de leur fonction sociale' à cela il ajoute 'notre joie esthéti-

* Oublié des Européens et peut-être irréalisable. Rattray dit que certains mots d'Ashanti ont des sens qui ne sont pas traduisibles.
Rattray, *Ashanti.*

que peut être grandement accrue par l'étude de la vie et des mœurs qui donnèrent naissance à ces œuvres.' Mais malheur à ceux qui, par sympathie et pour accroître leurs connaissances, se tourneraient vers *The Golden Bough* de Frazer! Il y passa bien des années de sa vie à compiler, trier et classer des documents sur les mœurs, coutûmes et croyances primitives. Dans sa préface à *Aftermath,* supplément de *The Golden Bough* il dit: 'Je fus entraîné comme par quelque subtil enchanteur à rédiger ce que je ne puis considérer qu'une chronique sombre et tragique d'erreurs et de folies humaines, d'entreprises stériles, de temps perdu, d'espoirs brisés.' Il conclut 'tout au plus cette chronique peut servir d'avertissement, comme une sorte de fil d'Ariane qui aidera le malheureux voyageur à éviter certains des pièges et des trappes où ses camarades sont tombés avant lui dans le labyrinthe de la vie.' Pourtant, en présence du plaisir esthétique très réel que nous ressentons devant l'art de l'Afrique Occidentale nous ne pouvons renoncer à l'espoir du Professeur Olbrecht, pour nous laisser aller au désespoir de Frazer. Il nous faut décider que même si les croyances et les coutûmes de l'homme primitif peuvent être erronées, sa foi en lue-même, exprimée dans son art, est juste, quelle que soit la manière inadéquate dont il décrive ses croyances et ses mœurs. Le plaisir esthétique que donne son art doit rester un mystère entre nous-mêmes et l'art, et ne doit pas être confondu avec son milieu. Car c'est seulement si ces deux éléments (la permanence de l'art et le mutabilité de la vie) restent distincts que nous pouvons entretenir l'espoir de réconcilier les opinions opposées (espoir et désespoir) sur la valeur de l'art du passé.

Abstraction pure et religieuse.

Ces œuvres retiennent un sens esthétique même si les coutûmes et croyances qui leur ont donné naissance sont mortes. Ainsi, quels que soient le dogme et la doctrine, ils semblent futiles tant que la foi est présente. Une croyance abstraite sans dogme ni doctrine n'était pas possible à l'africain non plus que—eût elle été possible—elle n'aurait donné à son art l'expression individuelle, l'attrait pour tous, ni la puissance unifiante qui amena les tribus à se former. L'expression individuelle et l'attrait pour tous sont les attributs de tout art grand et durable. Malgré les mélancoliques imperfections de ses mœurs et de ses croyances, la société africaine était une union dont les racines étaient dans le sol. Parlant des bois sacrés, Frazer dit: 'Tout cela, la plantation, l'arbre, la pierre représentent la terre, mère sacrée de toutes choses.' Dans le culte de Shongo des Yorubes, qui furent pendant un temps, une tribu qui exerça une influence extensive sur la Nigeria, le motif le plus fréquemment mis en usage par l'artiste pour invoquer les esprits qui dispensent la fertilité est celui de la mère et de l'enfant: notre mère, la terre, nourrissant l'humanité. Chaque membre de la tribu en Afrique s'identifié avec l'humanité, les animaux et même les arbres, en tant qu'enfants de la terre. Il n'est pas difficile d'accepter l'importance de sa croyance chez un africain, car il est impossible de concevoir quelle attitude envers la vie il aurait eue sans foi, même s'il avait su que bientôt son dogme et sa doctrine allaient être mis en doute. Le sculpteur dotait cette croyance d'une expression vitale. Dans une langue qui avait cours il créait des images représentant les esprits qui donnaient la fertilité, premier principe qui assurait sa bien-être, celui de sa famille et de sa tribu.

Dans le cas du chrétien, sa foi est en elle-même une abstraction qui retire tout contrôle aux esprits de la foi primitive et le place en grande partie dans la conscience du croyant. Cette foi demande une représentation artistique du type idéal de l'homme pour abriter l'idéal abstrait de la conscience. Les madones sont des représentations de la femme idéale, non d'esprits. Pour le primitif, la religion et l'art sont des aspects de la vie qu'on ne doit pas considérer séparément. Pour lui, l'objet de l'art c'est de réprésenter ou de refléter, en plaisant à tous, le monde invisible des esprits avec leurs caractéristiques et leurs identités séparées, régissant les conditions du bien-être de l'homme par la fertilité de la terre. La femme, représentant notre mère, la terre, est inspirée d'un type humble et commun non idéalisé. Dans un tel cadre, l'art abstrait, tout comme la *musique* pure de l'Occident, ne pouvait exister, en tant que création, distinct du goût et des méthodes communs.

La conception occidentale d'abstraction pure dans les arts visuels provient de la promotion intellectuelle des esprits qui régissaient l'Afrique en atomes et électrons qui se livrent à leurs affaires légitimes et impersonnelles, tout en gouvernant un univers impersonnel.

Il suit logiquement que, en transgressant sa foi, l'homme de la tribu africaine n'offense pas sa conscience mais les esprits du monde invisible dont la colère non apaisée les pousserait à exercer leur vengeance sur lui, sa famille ou la tribu entière. Le monde externe a été dénué d'esprits par l'occidental qui a renfermé toutes ses valeurs spirituelles dans sa conscience. Le vague qui s'attache à l'attrait de toutes ces entités dont le siége est la conscience leur a fait perdre leur popularité.

Les leprechauns peuvent encore se rencontrer en Irlande, mais ils n'inspirent plus ni assez de frayeur, ni assez de respect pour qu'on les honore d'une expression créatrice. Il semble clair que la foi doive être aussi forte que les émotions d'amour ou de crainte pour produire un art religieux dont la puissance créatrice, réglée par un jeu d'émotions variées, fasse appel à tout le monde—quelle que soit la direction que lui donne la pensée.

Antiquité, climat, matériaux, tradition.

La question de l'ancienneté des œuvres d'art est rendue difficile par l'obscurité générale du *continent noir*. Roger Bacon a dit qu'il n'y avait qu'une seule obscurité et que c'était l'ignorance. Dans un territoire qui ne possède pas de récits écrits et où la mention d'une défaite militaire était défendue sous peine de mort, on ne peut donner aux œuvres d'art aucun ordre chronologique. C'est pourquoi on doit regarder l'art d'Afrique de la même façon que l'art préhistorique, sans siècles ni décades, en termes d'évolution.*

Un pays d'une vaste superficie où la faune et la flore sont abondantes est habité par l'homme qui a atteint un étage avancé dans le développement primitif. Un climat clément et la fertilité du sol ont une influence modératrice sur l'évolu-

* L'essai fait par un marchand parisien de dater les œuvres d'art en termes de siècles doit être regardé comme une pure fantaisie tant que ces œuvres ne subissent pas d'influence européenne.

tion des habitants. L'agriculture fit des progrès mais l'élevage des troupeaux fut empêché par la mouche tsé-tsé. Dans les tribus, il y eut d'innombrables mouvements de révolte en ferment, libérant ou réprimant tout à tour des influences intérieures variées. L'Afrique absorba toutes les influences extérieures sans rien perdre à cause d'elles, avant la pénétration opérée par la science et l'industrialisme occidentaux. Une certaine immunité contre le paludisme fut acquise par les habitants, qui les aida beaucoup à se défendre contre les envahisseurs étrangers. L'archéologue a des surprises en découvrant des signes d'intrusions et d'influences étrangères qui ont disparu sans plus laisser de traces.*

L'humidité du climat corrode toutes substances et la fourmi blanche ou termite est un destructeur du bois très rapide. Il est regrettable que le bois soit la matière par excellence dont travaille le sculpteur et dont se nourrit la fourmi blanche dans un pays qui ne possède pas de pierre se prêtant facilement à la sculpture. Mais il est possible que ce fait ait contribué à préserver l'art des adeptes du culte des dieux lares du danger du style statique de la pierre. Le bois étant périssable ne permettait à aucune œuvre d'assumer un caractère de durée et ceci ajouta à la variété de styles et au dynamisme si caractérisque de l'art de l'Afrique Occidentale. Mais la question est de savoir si la vie de tribu en petits groupements se serait soumise à la tradition statique même si elle avait convenu au tempérament de l'africain. Une ressource abondante de pierre durable aurait eu néanmoins quelque influence stabilisatrice sur un style que nous trouvons si spontané. En effet supposons que les sculptures égyptiennes de porphyre se soient écroulées en quelques années à cause du climat et de la fourmi blanche, aucun des gigantesques pharaons ne se serait dressé au-dessus des déserts prohibant aux dynasties à venir tout variation, sauf les plus superficielles, dans l'art antique, majesteux et révéré de l'Egypte. La diversité extraordinaire des sculptures africaines, bien qu'en grande partie dùe au caractère de la race a dù trouver quelque appui dans la corruptibilité des matériaux limités.

* Les têtes de bronze de Ife; les statues steatites d'Essie et les terres suites de Jemme, pour ne mentionner que la Nigeria.

L'abstraction de la forme en Afrique.

Je ne peux trouver de terme plus juste pour définir l'abstraction dans la sculpture nègre que celui de forme *pré-logique*. Quel que soit le terme employé, il faut aussi qu'il soit valide pour décrire l'abstraction que l'on trouve sous sa forme naissante dans les dessins d'enfant. L'adulte nègre conserve l'impulsion initiale qu'a l'enfant pour s'exprimer. Les dessins d'enfant ont une simplicité naïve qui s'apparente au caractère humain de l'œuvre nègre. Ils sont tous les deux exempts de timidité, quoique ni l'un ni l'autre ne croie que le monde sensible qui l'entoure ressemble aux représentations qu'il en donne. 'Si vous ne devenez de petits enfants . . .' sans cette innocence cette simplicité de l'enfant qui ne met rien en doute, on rendra un hommage exagéré à ces traits secondaires qui mettent obstacle a l'expression de la foi— Roger Fry a dit dans *The Art of the Bushmen*:* 'Les dessins primitifs de notre race ressemblent étrangement à ceux des enfants. Leur caractère le plus frappant est leur dépendance des concepts du langage. Dans un dessin d'enfant on trouve un certain nombre de formes qui ne répondent guère à des apparences réelles, mais qui symbolisent directement la conception la plus significative de la chose représentée. Pour un enfant la conception d'un homme se résume en la tête (qui à son tour consiste en yeux, nez et bouche), les bras, les mains (cinq doigts), les jambes et les pieds. Le torse ne l'intéresse pas et il est par conséquent réduit en général à une seule ligne qui semble constituer le lien entre le symbole du concept tête et les jambes. L'enfant sait naturellement que le corps ainsi dessiné n'est pas comme celui de l'homme mais c'est une sorte de hiéroglyphe de l'homme, et cela satisfait son désir d'expression.' Il convient de reconnaître la perspicacité des observations de Fry sur la similarité entre les dessins de l'enfant et de l'homme de la forêt. Leur dessin est d'un style appelé schématisme. On peut l'expliquer, comme le suggère Fry, comme une sorte de naturalisme abrégé ou une déclara-

* *The Art of the Bushmen—Vision and Design* par Roger Fry. Article réimprimé dans le BURLINGTON MAGAZINE de 1910.

tion faite en sténographie ou *signe hieroglyphique.* Ce qu'il ne faut pas confondre avec l'abstraction faite par le nègre que j'ai appelée forme pré-logique. La manière dont le nègre interprète le torse est aussi directe que celle de l'enfant dessinant la tête (avec les yeux, le nez et la bouche) mais elle n'est pas si simple ni si grossière. Il s'intéresse à ces caractères du torse qui donnent une expression à sa croyance: le nombril —le cordon ombilical, les seins en saillie de la mère—qui entretiennent la vie de l'enfant; le pubis—portail de la vie, et les cicatrices et les signes distinctifs de la tribu sur le corps —passeport qui lui permettra de rejoindre les esprits de ses compagnons de tribu dans la vie de l'au-delà. En insistant sur ces traits et en les élargissant tout en les simplifiant il cherche à donner au torse l'aspect divin qui distingue le seuil du monde surnaturel. Les surfaces planes du torse et les membres avec leurs ondulations superficielles et subtiles ne lui disent rien. Son seul usage de ses parties du corps est de diminuer les formes conceptuelles pour arriver à exprimer les traits capitaux et les amener à former une nouvelle unité qui représente un esprit: dans cet esprit il voit, reflété dans le monde sensible, le monde surnaturel.

Un enfant ignore tout des caractéristiques du torse. Il dessine les organes des sens de la tête, car pour lui ils représentent le monde sensible et mystérieux où il entre graduellement avec l'aide des adultes. L'enfant ne confondrait pas le visage d'un autre avec celui de sa mère. Il est conscient de la subtilité des traits qui distinguent une tête d'une autre mais ces traits n'ont encore aucun sens pour lui. Le petit européen acquiert bientôt une conscience pour se comporter correctement envers les esprits qui habitent le monde spirituel du nègre. Par l'intérêt qu'il porte aux contes des fées et dans ses rapports intimes avec ses jeunes compagnons, il montre qu'il a hérité de ses ancêtres la tendance à peupler d'esprits le monde sensible. Ni l'enfant, ni le sculpteur nègre ne s'intéressent intellectuellement à la notion de forme, autrement ils ne pourraient en user si librement ni se soucier si peu du sort de leur œuvre. L'enfant délaisse et détruit son travail, et le primitif celui des ennemis qu'il a vaincus—quelle que soit la valeur esthétique de l'œuvre.

Pourtant la sculpture du nègre ne pourrait surpasser le dessin de l'enfant par son fini ou sa finalité comme elle le fait, si le nègre ne portait pas quelque intérêt à la forme.

La nature de son intimité avec la forme est peut-être mieux décrite par le mot analogie. Pour lui la forme est le gage d'une valeur indirecte—comparable à celle que nous attachons à la formule d'un chèque; c'est quelque chose de très important dans le détail mais qui n'a aucune valeur s'il n'y a un crédit en banque pour le couvrir. Personne, si ce n'est dans une école de comptabilité, ne fait ni ne reçoit de chèques pour le plaisir d'en faire. Les chèques sont notre fétiche—comme la sculpture pour le nègre—mais jamais notre idole. L'art nègre est une représentation créatrice, tel le dessin de l'enfant, qui a pour un temps le pouvoir de lui donner une impression d'emprise sur quelque chose d'invisible qu'il obtient en tirant l'abstraction de quelque chose de vu. Quand l'enfant, le sculpteur noir et nos banquiers se servent d'une manière indirecte de la forme, toutes ses valeurs sont mises au service de l'expression; la nécessité pressante d'expression est telle qu'aucune technique n'a le droit de s'interposer.

Les grammairiens de la forme (pour paraphraser un terme emprunté au domaine des langues*) viennent plus tard qui rendent cette expression consciente d'elle-même grâce à la technique avec des nuances subtiles de sens. Ceci se produit quand le feu de l'enthousiasme initial est réduit à des cendres rougeoyantes.

L'ecole africaine.

Les écoles des beaux-arts de l'Afrique Occidentale constituaient ses sociétés secrètes. Le capitaine F. W. Butt-Thompson, parlant d'elles dans ses *Societiés secrètes d'Afrique Occidentale*—'Elles furent instituées pour maintenir en

---

* Philologie: étude des langues par rapport à l'action morale et intellectuelle des peuples qui s'en servent; mais le sens le plus répandu maintenant est science du langage; science linguistique souvent définie par le titre comparatif de philologie comparée (Concise English Dictionary). L'étude intellectuelle de la forme devient aussi détachée de la necessité où elle était originellement employée dans le domaine de l'art qu'elle l'est dans le domaine de langues.

vigeur les traditions de la tribu, ses coutûmes et ses croyances qui étaient en danger de changer ou de tomber en désuétude. Les organisateurs étaient des champions de l'ancien contre le nouveau, comme le sont encore certains de leurs descendants. Ils restreignaient le progrès mental et punissaient les hérétiques. Ils étaient assez intelligents pour savoir que la prohibition seule ne suffisait pas pour fonder une société désirant être assurée de longévité et par conséquent firent de leurs sociétés les sanctuaires des légendes, des mythes, de l'histoire et des conceptions d'art et de culture, de connaissances et de sagesse que la tribu possédait. De plus, ils se mirent à enseigner toutes ces choses—et ils en étaient les seuls pédagogues.'

De telles institutions primitives protégèrent les arts et les développèrent en les rendant populaires. Sous leur influence les arts furent florissants tant que leur puissance conservatrice grandit mais du moment où leur expansion cessa et que le conservatisme devint absolu et statique, les arts déclinèrent. La formule de leur sagesse était l'interprétation et la personnification des esprits du monde invisible dans un culte qui survécut longtemps dans l'isolement où était l'Afrique. L'art exprimait leurs émotions religieuses sous une forme organisée et retenue. Les premiers explorateurs européens qui allèrent en Afrique Occidentale y trouvèrent un art épanoui qu'ils ne comprirent pas. Eux et les premiers missionnaires n'attachèrent aucune valeur aux mœurs et croyances païennes qui soit comparable au christianisme et détruisirent bien des choses dans leur zèle à châtier et à convertir.

On ne peut faire aucun commentaire positif là-dessus. Ce qui fut conservé par curiosité ou par intérêt scientifique dût attendre bien longtemps en Europe—un sens plus éclectique de la tradition—que l'on reconnaisse sa portée spirituelle.

La pénétration économique de l'Afrique par l'Europe coupa court à toute continuation d'évolution. Qui peut savoir si l'Afrique Occidentale de l'avenir—son peuple étant pourvu d'une conscience européenne au lieu d'une phalange de mentors spirituels—ne trouvera pas une forme nouvelle d'expression artistique ?

La connaissance de la forme du sculpteur était limitée au volume et à la surface. Il savait comment faire rendre à sa matière* les émotions de sa foi simple. Nous ne voyons pas l'artiste dans ses statues essayer d'explorer l'espace en arrangeant ses formes autour d'un axe en spirale; les colonnes vertébrales de ses statues ne sont jamais représentées en rotation ce qui donnerait différents angles, une variété de contours,† qu'on les regarde de face, de côté ou de dos. La tête tourne rarement sur le cou. On ne peut regarder ces sculptures que de deux façons, de face et de côté. Il est curieux et peut-être significatif de remarquer que l'enfant, dans les sculptures de *mère et enfant* fait exception. Dans les œuvres provenant, soit du Yorubaland, soit du Congo belge, l'enfant est représenté dans une attitude plus abandonnée qui contraste avec la raideur droite de sa mère. Généralement parlant, la rigidité de pose que l'on trouve dans les sculptures africaines laisse toute suggestion de mouvement à la variété subtile des formes et des surfaces.

La cosmogonie de l'Afrique primitive ne s'étend pas aux espaces libres qui dépassent les forêts tropicales et par-dessus son ciel bleu profond si variable, que l'on regarde comme un plan solide, un plafond—l'Afrique, par son art, reflète les frontières limitées de son monde sensible; le dos, le devant, les côtés des statues—les quatre vents; les pieds et la tête-terre et ciel. Les lieux obscurs où l'esprit africain a pu battre la campagne ne suscitèrent aucune exploration de son imagination qui l'ait poussé à faire des recherches sur la forme sculpturelle.

---

* La plupart de ses œuvres étaient en bois (ce qui constitue le sujet de ce volume) mais il avait un sens artistique égal quelle que soit la matière dont il se servit.

† De notables exceptions à cette observation sont des statues de pierre (les nomalies steatites et les dieux de riz) de la Sierra Leone. Elles sont d'origine très ancienne et probablement dûes à une influence étrangère. D'autres exceptions telles que les soldats portugais et les arquebusiers en bronze de Benin sont aussi acceptées comme appartenant à un style introduit.

INDEX AND DESCRIPTIVE NOTES
TO THE PLATES

1. BISAGOS ISLES, Length approx. 20 ins. A food-bowl, supported on the game-carrying poles of a hunting people; the dog on the lid aiding in tracking and retrieving the quarry. *Author's collection.*

2A. MENDE, Bo district, Sierra Leone. Height 12 ins. *In possession of Government Training College, Bo.*

2B. MENDE, Sierra Leone. Height 46 ins. Blackened. *British Museum.*

3A. MENDE, Sierra Leone. Height 19 ins. Blackened. *British Museum.*

3B. MENDE, Sierra Leone. Height 18 ins. Blackened. *In possession of Government Training College, Bo.*

3C. MENDE, Sierra Leone. Height 17 ins. Blackened. *British Museum.*

Female figures of the Mende show great expression of a human kind, varying from a resigned piety to a geniality which approaches humour. The Mende made few male figures in wood.

4. MENDE, Sierra Leone, height 22 ins. Probably a Bundu society carving: blackened. *Author's collection.*

5. SHERBO, Coastal Area, Sierra Leone. Height 18 ins. Palmwood. *British Museum.*

The body is hollow beneath the neck and the head detachable. The style of the head is particularly reminiscent of the steatite 'nomalies' and rice gods of more ancient origin, found beneath the surface in Sierra Leone.

6. BAMBARA, French Sudan. Height 30 ins. Female carrier in two respects: of water(?); and of the progeny. One of the infrequent examples of African assymetrical composition. *British Museum.*

7. BAMBARA, French Sudan. Height 24 ins. Blackened. *British Museum.*

   Style shows some affinity to the Mende figures of Sierra Leone.

8A BAMBARA-MALI, French Sudan. Height (a) 18 ins., (b) 14 ins.
& B. Figure Bambara (a) has been compared with the figure (b) of the Yoruba carver Bamboye—which has been introduced to illustrate the degeneration under Western influence. The Bambara figure (a) has lost its surface, by erosion, yet retains the more lively disposition of sculptural mass, which (b) lacks.

9. SENUFO, Ivory Coast. Height 13 ins. Mounted man (warrior?) with rifle. The relative proportions of body, head, and legs of man descending, as the proportion of man to his mount. *British Museum.*

10. BAULE, Ivory Coast. Height 18 ins. Hardwood dark. *Royal Scottish Museum, Edinburgh.*

    Ancestor figure. Enthroned (?). Compare with the fetish figure of the Lower Congo (Plate 43B). The attitude in both is that of repose and conservation of energy, but its rendering in these two figures is very different from that of similar attitude in early Demeters of Greece and the Pharoahs of Egypt. In these latter it expresses absolute stasis.

11. BAULE, Gold Coast. Height 11 ins. and 12 ins. *Collection of R. P. Bedford, Esq.*

    From the necklet of the female of these two ancestor figures is suspended a Victorian sixpence dated 1901.

12. BAULE, Ivory Coast. Height 11 ins. The calm sculptural dignity of some Baule figures is well exemplified in this one. *Author's collection.*

13. ASHANTI, Ghana. Height about 14 ins. Ossesi wood. *Collection M. Cockin, Esq.*

    The executioner. The Ashantis were not great carvers of figures, and those they made usually relate to their military might and austere justice; executioners, prisoners and captors and incidents from Ashanti life.

14A. ASHANTI, Gold Coast. Height about 11 ins. Blackened. *British Museum.*

14B. ASHANTI, Gold Coast. Height about 11 ins. Blackened. *Collection W. O. Oldman, Esq.*

Known as Akabas or dolls and carried by women desiring a child. The large head with regular features and long thin neck are Ashanti points of beauty which it is desirable the expected child should possess. Only those features of the body which are associated with reproduction and fertility are represented on a cylindrical torso with arms merely indicated by stumps.

15. FON, Dahomey, length of lions 8 ins. A detail carved on the shaft of a ritual object. A fairy-tale grimness in the scene, man as the meal of two lions.

16A. YORUBA, Southern Nigeria. Height, 27 ins. Head-dress coloured & B. indigo, figure red (tukula). *In possession of the author.*

Yoruba woman personifying *The Earth Feeding Mankind.* The colouring of this figure is obviously symbolical—the red earth of Africa. The advanced primitive style of the Yorubas in this work recalls that of the Byzantine school which returned to the directness of primitive art.

17A. YORUBA (Northern), Southern Nigeria. Height 15 ins. Head-& B. dress coloured indigo. *Collection of Rene d'Harnoncourt, Esq., N.Y.*

The fertility motive in a Shongo priest's staff. Pendulous and heavy-laden breasts have become a point of beauty, recalling the representation of women in an advanced stage of pregnancy in Flemish art of the 15th Century. African women sometimes bandage their breasts to produce this effect.

18. YORUBA-IFA, Western Nigeria. Height 9 ins. A horseman supporting a bowl as a receptacle for the palm-kernels used in Ifa divination of the Yorubas. This example reaches the peak of Yoruba carvers' mastery, in subordinating all detail to the unity of the mass. *Author's collection.*

19. Another view of Plate 18.

20A. YORUBA, Southern Nigeria. Height 15 ins. *Royal Scottish Museum, Edinburgh.*

A Shongo priest's staff.

20B. YORUBA, Southern Nigeria. Height 21 ins. Coloured: figure, indigo; robe, painted with pattern of native weaving in indigo and red (tukula). *In possession of the author.*

Compare the enlarged head of this figure with the reduced head of the mother in Plate 16. In this figure (Plate 20b) woman is represented in her biological role—human fertility; whereas in Plate 16 she personifies, with her child *mankind,* a more comprehensive idea of fertility—that of the earth. The association of the idea of woman as mother of the race with mother of the universe (the earth of Africa) is emphasized in sculptural expressions by a reduction of the head, thereby giving a monumental scale to the body.

21A, YORUBA (Northern), Southern Nigeria. Height 9 to 11 ins. *In B, C. possession of the author.*

These little Yoruba figures are known as Ibegi twins, possessed by Yorubas who have lost a twin by death. A figure of the same sex is carried or kept in the house to appease the spirit of the dead child, so that should it return it may not find the living twin companionless and take it away.

22. YORUBA, Western Nigeria, Height 10 ins. A figure of the type known as *ibejis* or twins. A great variety of style exists in different parts of Yorubaland. *Author's collection.*

23A. YORUBA, Southern Nigeria. Height 9 ins. *In possession of the & B. author.*

The enlargement of the head is a pervading characteristic of these twin figures.

24. YORUBA, Western Nigeria, Height 19 ins. A fine example of Yoruba style and favourite subject-matter in this piece, and plate 18 above. *British Museum.*

25A. IGALA, Southern Nigeria. Height 72 ins. Iroko wood. Coloured & B. with native pigments and trade ultramarine. *Collection W. O. Oldman, Esq.*

The art form of this work, termed an 'Ikeng' figure, is that of the totem pole. The long-eared tribal spirit personified at the top is smoking a pipe. Beneath it are various attributes represented by figures and objects. In the middle section, supporting the tribal spirit, is woman representing human fertility and, at the base, a pipe-smoking executioner or perhaps head-hunter.

26. URHOBO, Southern Nigeria. Height 42 ins. Iroko wood, coloured similarly to Plate 25. *Collection W. O. Oldman, Esq.*

The treatment of this is not wholly a composition of several forms, as in Plate 25, but a combining only of the significant features of such forms for the achievement of a new unity. The cockatrice of Europe is a survival of this idea. The fanged maw and legs of the animal at the base are those of the leopard. The leopard's head is reduced to a fanged mouth, mounted directly without body on legs. The legs are painted with leopard's spots. Does it mean ferocious speed or swift ferocity? The head of the divinity or spirit in the centre is attended on each side by baboon-like figures with human-faced birds (messengers?) on their heads, the divinity being surmounted by a composite and human-faced animal. The subject of the piece seems, with its tribal totem above, to be based upon fleet ferocity.

27A. IBIBIO. Uyo district, Southern Nigeria. Height 10 ins. Black-
& B. ened. *British Museum.*

A linear groove defines clothing on body, cheekbones and eyebrows of 27a. Enrichment of the plain surface of the bodies by increased relief of significant features (nipples, umbilicus, genitals and kneecaps), brings the bodies into a sculptural balance with the heads.

28. IDOMA, Northern Nigeria. Height 12 ins. The thighs have been given more axial variation, to continue the interest of the head, lower down. *Author's collection.*

29. IDOMA, Northern Nigeria. Height 20 ins. Blackened. *Horniman's Museum.*

Mother and Child. The simple ascending mass and enlargement of the mother's head in this group points to its motive as representing the dignity of human fertility.

30. AFO, Northern Nigeria. Height about 24 ins. Blackened. *Horniman's Museum.*

The dignity of motherhood. The sculptured treatment suggests a multiplicity of children; more than the three represented.

31A. TIV, Northern Nigeria. Height 48 ins. Hardwood dark. *Collection of R. P. Bedford, Esq.*

31B. TIV, Northern Nigeria. Height 36 ins. *Horniman's Museum.*

These figures have the same air of pious humility as the Mende figure, Plate 2b.

32A. BAMUM, Cameroons. Height (a) 10 ins. (b) 11 ins. Two of the
& B. changes, which this tribe rings on the figures of this type. *British Museum.*

33. ASHANI, North-Eastern Nigeria. Height 35 ins. *British Museum.*
There is a resemblance in the broad sculptural treatment of this
figure with the Ashani figure of Plate 34; but there is also a delicacy
and refinement of line such as result only from a tradition of long
development, yet there are no known figures of the same provenance to this one. It has some distant, generic resemblance to
the many hundred steatite figures discovered in an old sacred grove
at Essie, Southern Nigeria, in 1931.

34. ASHANI, North-Eastern Nigeria. Height about 24 ins. Blackened.
The features of the head picked out in white (kaolin). *British Museum.*
The sculptured features of the torso are those connected with
fertility (sex, navel and nipples). A gentle spiral movement, like
that suggested in vegetation, is imparted by the arrangement of
planes in the arms, and is heightened by the slight cast of the head
to the left. It gives the figure the impression of being planted on
the soil and aspiring to the light and air.

35. FANG, Gaboon. Height 10 ins. Brass pupils to the eyes. *Collection of Robert Sainsbury, Esq.*
Ancestor spirit represented by the head alone. Abstractions of
the natural form of the head are carved in such a way as if drawn
out in some elastic material, giving the head a wraith-like aspect.
One feels it must relate to a gentle spirit.

36A. FANG, Gaboon. Height 24 ins. Originally had metal plates
applied. *In possession of Blair Hughes-Stanton, Esq.*
The sensitive form of this figure conveys a spirit-like gentleness
in the subject similar to Plate 35.

36B. Detail of Plate 36A.

37. FANG, Gaboon. Height approx. 18 ins. In the same tribal style
as the classical Gaboon head (Plates 35 and 36). The subjective
variation of natural proportion is more sensitive than in most
African styles. *British Museum.*

44

38A. FANG, Gaboon. Height 24 ins. Plates of thin brass applied. *Horniman's Museum.*

This figure has some affinity with the Fang figures of Plates 38b and 36a.

38B. FANG, Gaboon. Height 25 ins. *In possession of B. Hughes-Stanton, Esq.*

The head of a child on its mother's back is invariably turned to one side. Whenever the frontal direction of the head is varied in African figures, it is given a full quarter turn. No lesser turn occurs. R. E. Dennett, discussing African cosmogony, says that the Yorubas lived in a square universe.

39. BAKOTA, Ogowe district, French Congo. Height about 30 ins. Overlaid with repoussé copper and brass. *British Museum.*

The body of the ancestor is reduced to a mere lozenge, a form which has some special significance for the tribe, as cryptograms, in various forms of lozenge, appear in relief on the reverse of these Bakota figures.

40. BAKONGO (Bass Congo). Height 21 ins. Prophet, lawgiver, or functionary of commanding aspect: obviously wearing the European (Belgian?) frock-coat with tails and breeches. The posture is reminiscent of the Bakuta figures of Congo kings; see Plate 49. *Author's collection.*

41. LOWER CONGO. Height 18 ins. *In possession of Miss Gertrude Hermes.*

The deified spirit of intoxication (?).

42. LOWER CONGO. Height 36 ins. *Horniman's Museum.*

A nail fetish. Expression is concentrated in the head. The body is kept plain to receive the nails of devotees; instruments of sympathetic magic.

43A. BABEMBE, Belgian Congo. Height 9 ins. *British Museum.*

Emphasis is given to the feet and the tribal cicatrization of the body in these small figures of Babembe. See Plate 44.

43B. LOWER CONGO. Height 6 ins. *In possession of James Keggie, Esq.* A fetish figure.

44. BABEMBE, Belgian Congo. Height 5½ ins. *British Museum.*

45. KUYU, Mid-Congo. Height 28 ins. Blackened and coated with gum. *In possession of Blair Hughes-Stanton, Esq.*

The form has great stability and repose. It may be a fetish figure of oracle. The mouth is depicted as if about to speak. There is no receptacle for medicine in the figure but it may have been applied to the surface with the gum.

46. BAYAKA, Belgian Congo. Height 14 ins. Brass-headed nails in forehead. *The Royal Scottish Museum, Edinburgh.*

A fetish figure with enlarged feet conveying the idea of firm contact with the earth.

47. BASUKU-BAYAKA, Belgian Congo. Height 6 ins. In a style which is influenced by the subject-matter of the Bayaka tribe (Plate 46). *Author's collection.*

48. BAJOKWE, Angola, Spanish West Africa. Height 11 ins. *Collection of R. P. Bedford, Esq.*

The soldier-raider-hunter needs large able hands and firm feet.

49. BAMBALA, sub-tribe of the Bushongo. King Shamba Bolongongo of the Belgian Congo. Height 24 ins. *British Museum.*

The famous statues of the Congo rulers are more portrayals of an ideal type than of individuals. They have rather less variation of individual features than the bronze heads of Benin and considerably less than those of Ife.

50. BANGENDI, sub-tribe of the Bushongo, Sankura River, Belgian Congo. Height 10 ins. *British Museum.*

Collected by Torday and described as a 'house charm.' Features selected for emphasis in this figure of a female spirit are head, hands and feet (foreparts missing). The features of the torso are grouped closely to present a sort of visage, secondary to that of the face.

51. BAWONGO-BUSHONGO, Lower Belgian Congo. Height 13 ins. A ceremonial hoe: the revered iron on the blade is given great length from the mouth of the figure—probably an agricultural divinity—with a bird of unknown import on his back. *British Museum.*

52A. BENA LULUA, Belgian Congo. Height 10 ins. A, *Collection W. O. Oldman, Esq.*: B, *in possession of J. Keggie, Esq.*
& B.

The tribal markings, passports to tribal quarters in the life hereafter, are given prominence in these elaborate and sensitive little figures. Note the projection of the navel cord in Fig. B; the thread which at birth connects man with the spirit world whence he came.

53. BASONGE, Belgian Congo. Height 22 ins. Blue bead necklace. *Collection W. O. Oldman, Esq.*

Both head and torso in different degrees are compressed in volume for the more dominant display of their respective enlarged features. The enlarged head, hands, and feet are significant—the feet especially, of a grip on the earth. Beauty demands the extraction of the front teeth.

54. BASONGE, South-Eastern Congo. Height 22 ins. Another instance of the assymetrical composition (see Plate 6), with a fetish-horn on the head, and ornamentation of brass-headed studs. The transverse axis of the head gives more naturalism. *British Museum.*

55. BASONGE-BATETELA, South-Eastern Congo. Height 10 ins. A columnar composition of the figure, electing the face, sternum, and arms for abstract prominence. *Author's collection.*

56. BALUBA, South-Eastern Congo. Height 20 ins. One of the finest of the celebrated stools, supported by the kneeling female caryatid. *British Museum.*

57. BALUBA, South-Eastern Congo. Length 11 ins. Ceremonial bowl; blackened. *Author's collection.*

58. URUA, Belgian Congo. Height 12 ins. *British Museum.*

Limbs diminished and flexed to give prominence and straightness to head and torso is typical of Urua figures.

59. BALUBA, Belgian Congo. Height 29 ins. *Collection W. O. Oldman, Esq.*

A full stomach and a large head are elected as significant and supported on sturdy legs by large feet. A fine appreciation of the thrust of the pelvis on the head of the trocanter is made to give effect to the weight of the stomach.

60. BALUBA, South-Eastern Congo. Heights (A) 8 ins. (B) 7 ins. Two well-designed figures (in that they preserve the matrix-stick form from which they were carved). *Author's collection.*

61. BALUBA, Belgian Congo. Height 21 ins. Elaborate cicatrization on body, back and front. *Collection W. O. Oldman, Esq.*

A large cavity at the back of the head for the reception of medicine to consecrate and empower the fetish figure in the service of the spirit personified by it.

62A. WABEMBE, Belgian Congo.   Height 8 ins.   *Collection W. O.*
& B. *Oldman, Esq.*

Male and female figures jugated at the head by a symbol of the
male and female organs of sex.

63. AZANDE, Extreme Eastern border of Congo.   Height 32 ins.

64. AZANDE, Extreme Eastern border of Congo.   Height 21 ins.
This style, and the Wabembe (plate 62), are at the easternmost
extremities of the Congo area.   They share a similarity; in contrast
with the generality of Congo styles.   *British Museum.*

*The revision for the new edition has been made with the valuable assistance of
Mr. W. B. Fagg in correcting the errors of provenance appearing in the
earlier editions.*

1. BISAGOS ISLES.   *Length approx. 20 ins.*

2A & B. MENDE, Sierra Leone. *Height 12 ins. and 46 ins.*

3A, B, C. MENDE, Sierra Leone. *Height 19 ins., 18 ins., 17 ins.*

4. MENDE, Sierra Leone. *Height 22 ins.*

5. SHERBO, Sierra Leone.
Height 18 ins.

6. BAMBARA, French Sudan.
Height 30 ins.

7. BAMBARA, French Sudan.
Height 24 ins.

8A & B. BAMBARA-MALI, French Sudan. *Height 18 ins. and 14 ins.*

9. SENUFO, Ivory Coast. *Height 13 ins.*

10. BAULE, Ivory Coast.
Height 18 ins.

11. BAULE, Gold Coast. *Height 11 ins. and 12 ins.*

12. BAULE, Ivory Coast.
Height 11 ins.

13. ASHANTI, Ghana. *Height about 14 ins.*

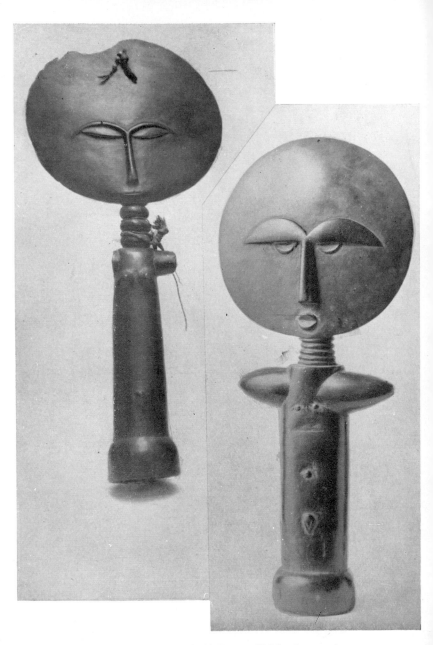

14A & B. ASHANTI, Gold Coast. *Height about 11 ins.*

15. FON, Dahomey. *Length of lions 8 ins.*

16A & B. YORUBA, Southern Nigeria. *Height 27 ins*.

17A & B. YORUBA (Northern), Southern Nigeria. *Height 15 ins.*

18. YORUBA-IFA, Western Nigeria. *Height 9 ins.*

19. Another view of plate 18.

20A & B. **YORUBA**, Southern Nigeria. *Height 15 ins. and 21 ins.*

21A, B, C. YORUBA (Northern),
Southern Nigeria. *Height 9 to 11 ins.*

22. YORUBA, Western Nigeria.
Height 10 ins.

23A & B. YORUBA, Southern Nigeria. *Height 9 ins.*

24. YORUBA, Western Nigeria. *Height 19 ins.*

25A & B. IGALA, Southern Nigeria. *Total height 72 ins.*

26. URHOBO, Southern Nigeria. *Height 24 ins.*

27A & B. IBIBIO, Uyo district, Southern Nigeria. *Height 10 ins.*

28. IDOMA, Northern Nigeria. *Height 12 ins.*

29. IDOMA, Northern Nigeria. *Height 20 ins.*

30. AFO, Norther Nigeria.
Height about 24 in

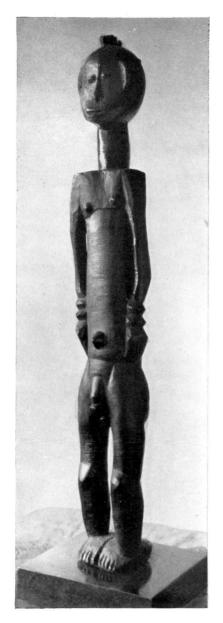

31A & B. TIV, Northern Nigeria. *A. Height 48 ins. B. Height 36 ins.*

32A & B. BAMUM, Cameroons. *Height (a) 10 ins.; (b) 11 ins.*

33. ASHANI, North-Eastern Nigeria.
Height 35 ins.

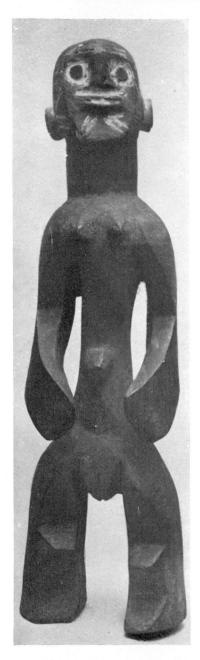

34. ASHANI, North-Eastern Nigeria.
Height about 24 ins.

35. FANG, Gaboon. *Height 10 ins.*

36A & B. FANG, Gaboon. *Total height 24 ins.*

37. FANG, Gaboon.
Height approx. 18 ins.

38A & B. FANG, Gaboon. *Height 24 ins. and 25 ins.*

39. BAKOTA, French Congo. *Height about 30 ins.*

40. BAKONGO, Bass Congo. *Height 21 ins.*

41. LOWER CONGO.
Height 18 ins.

42. LOWER CONGO.
Height 36 ins.

43A. BABEMBE, Belgian Congo. *Height 9 ins.*   43B. LOWER CONGO. *Height 6*

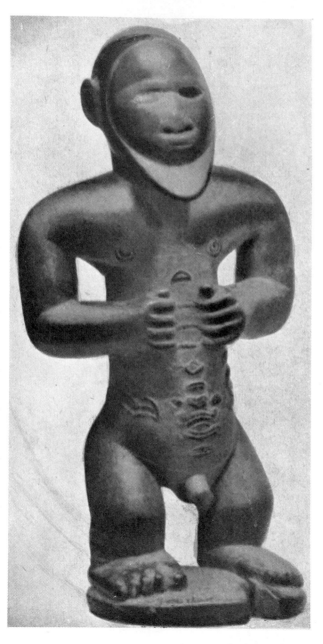

44. BABEMBE,
Belgian Congo.
Height 5½ ins.

45. KUYU, Mid-Congo.
Height 28 ins.

46. BAYAKA, Belgian Congo. *Height 14 ins.*

47. BASUKU-BAYAKA,
Belgian Congo.
Height 6 ins.

48. BAJOKWE, Angola. *Height 11 ins.*

49. BAMBALA, Belgian
Congo. *Height 24 ins.*

50. BAGENDI, Belgian
Congo. *Height 10 ins*.

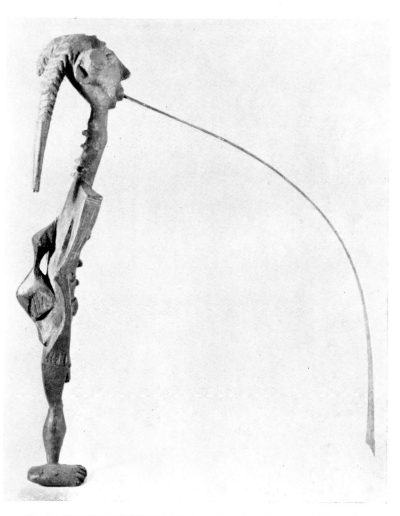

51. BAWONGO-BUSHONGO, lower Belgian Congo. *Height 13 ins.*

52. BENA LULUA, Belgian Congo. *Height 10 ins.*

53. BASONGE, Belgian
Congo. *Height 22 ins*.

54. BASONGE, South-
Eastern Congo.
Height 22 ins.

55. BASONGE-BATETELA,
South-Eastern Congo.
Height 10 ins.

56. BALUBA, South-Eastern Congo. *Height 20 ins.*

57. BALUBA, South-Eastern Congo. *Height 11 ins.*

58. URUA, Belgian Congo. *Height 12 ins.*

59. BALUBA, Belgian
Congo. *Height 29 ins.*

60. BALUBA, South-Eastern Congo. *Height (a) 8 ins.; (b) 7 ins.*

61. BALUBA, Belgian
Congo. *Height 21 ins.*

62. WABEMBA, Belgian
Congo. *Height 8 ins*.

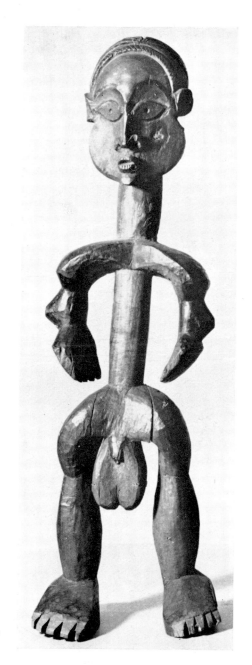

63. AZANDE, extreme
Eastern border of Congo.
Height 32 ins.

64. AZANDE, extreme Eastern
border of Congo. *Height 21 ins.*